At the Top of Their Game

Cam Newton

Trying to Win Them All

Jackie F. Stanmyre

Cavendish Square

New York

Published in 2018 by Cavendish Square Publishing, LLC
243 5th Avenue, Suite 136, New York, NY 10016

Library of Congress Cataloging-in-Publication Data

Names: Stanmyre, Jackie F.
Title: Cam Newton : trying to win them all / Jackie F. Stanmyre.
Description: New York : Cavendish Square, 2018. | Series: At the top of their game | Includes index.
Identifiers: ISBN 9781502628350 (library bound) | ISBN 9781502628381 (ebook)
Subjects: LCSH: Newton, Cam, 1989---Juvenile literature. | Football players--United States--Biography--Juvenile literature. | Quarterbacks (Football)--United States--Juvenile literature.
Classification: LCC GV939.N42 S73 2018 | DDC 796.332092--dc23

Editorial Director: David McNamara
Editor: Fletcher Doyle
Copy Editor: Rebecca Rohan
Associate Art Director: Amy Greenan
Designer: Jessica Nevins
Production Coordinator: Karol Szymczuk
Photo Research: J8 Media

Printed in the United States of America

At the Top of Their Game

Contents

Clearing Speed Bumps

Cam Newton lives in the spotlight of the National Football League. As the quarterback for the Carolina Panthers since 2011, Newton has broken numerous records that show off his talent both throwing and running with the football. In 2015, just his fourth year in the NFL, he was named the league's Most Valuable Player. He also led the Panthers to the Super Bowl that season, though the team lost. It has become clear over the years that losing is one of Newton's least favorite things to do. Some people have become critical of the way he handles defeat. One sportswriter called Newton "the loudest winner and the worst loser." Fortunately for Newton, he wins an awful lot more than he loses.

Because of his success, Newton is often at the center of the public's attention, with people watching his every move. In fact, Newton is such a big star that in 2015 he started a nationwide trend known as "dabbing," a dance move that entails extending his left arm, folding his right arm to his chest and ducking his head down toward his right elbow. Kids and adults across the country—including many other famous athletes and coaches—copied the dance they had seen Newton doing to celebrate **first downs** and touchdowns.

Opposite: Cam Newton has been the quarterback of the Carolina Panthers since 2011, when he was the first overall draft pick.

Cam Newton has become a cultural icon. He made popular a dance move known as "dabbing" during the 2015 NFL season.

While Newton may be a cultural icon now, his **divisiveness** is nothing new. Almost since the time he stepped foot on a football field, Newton has been a lightning rod for **scrutiny**. During a time when it became popular for high school athletes to create biographical highlight videos of themselves to show to college recruiters, Newton chose not to, saying simply, "My mentality was like, 'If you come see me, then I'll put on a show for you.' That wasn't cockiness or arrogance. That's just me speaking with confidence, saying that if you come see me, I'll hold myself accountable enough to play at a high level."

Newton was scouted by many college teams and ultimately chose to attend the University of Florida—but that's not where his college career ended. Because of some poor decisions he made in addition to on-field situations out of his control, Newton did not have a chance to star for the Gators. However, he didn't give up. He transferred to a two-year junior college named Blinn College, which he led to a national championship. Because of his success at Blinn, Newton caught the attention of the big-time coaches a second time and landed a second chance to play in the Southeastern Conference, among the best major college football conferences, with Auburn University. While at Auburn, Newton won a national championship and was awarded the Heisman Trophy, which is given annually to the most outstanding college football player. Newton was then drafted with the very first pick in the 2011 draft by the Carolina Panthers, for whom he has played ever since.

Despite the many successes he has experienced, Newton embodies the idea that the journey to the top will not be without its speed bumps. And yet, he continues to prove time and again that he will do what it takes to stay on top, and keep striving to go higher.

Chapter 1

Big Success

Cameron Jerrell Newton was born on May 11, 1989, in College Park, Georgia. He was the middle child born to Cecil and Jackie Newton, and he was groomed to be an athletic star from a young age. A natural athlete, Newton was drawn to many sports, but football was his earliest introduction to on-field competition. At age seven, Newton stepped on a football field for the first time.

Newton's father played football for Savannah State in the early 1980s. Cecil Newton was undersized but still good enough to get a chance to try out for two teams in the National Football League: the Dallas Cowboys and the Buffalo Bills. Wanting his sons to have a chance at the NFL career he always dreamed of, Cecil Newton had Cam and Cam's older brother Cecil Jr., practicing the game and going all-out in high-level drills before they were even teenagers.

Cam Newton was often the youngest player on the field, but also the biggest. He weighed ten pounds and nine ounces (4.8 kilograms) at birth, and his father said, "He has never had a small day in his life."

Opposite: Cam Newton (*top*) credits his parents, Cecil and Jackie Newton, with pushing him to succeed athletically and academically.

Some competitors asked to see his birth certificate, making him prove he was an appropriate age to compete. At least one of the leagues Newton competed in wasn't based on age—it was based on weight. By age eight, Newton stood close to five feet tall (1.5 meters) and weighed almost 100 pounds (45 kg). At times, Newton would skip meals to remain eligible for the team. While this decision wasn't good for his health, it showed that even early on, he was committed to doing whatever he could to be on the football field. Newton's size and **versatility** as an athlete was an ongoing theme throughout his childhood. He wasn't just big; he was very good, too.

After attending elementary school at Seaborn Lee, Newton moved on to Camp Creek Middle School. Newton was known for having endless energy in the classroom, which sometimes made it hard for him to focus on his schoolwork. Marie Caldwell, a teacher at Camp Creek, said learning came naturally to Newton. "It was difficult to get him to focus and settle down because he had a lot of energy. The same level of energy you see on the football field today is the same level we saw in the Camp Creek hallways. He was a child who liked to have a good time and laugh." But Newton's mother made sure he kept up in school. If he wanted to be able to play the games he loved so much, he would have to earn good grades, too. Later in life, Newton credited his mother for her support in his academic endeavors. "Everyone else has always been worried about the football side of things, but not my mother," Newton said. "My education was my mother's top priority. I've been blessed to have a family that supports me. It's a Biblical quote: Iron sharpens iron. My mother has always been there to sharpen me."

Focused on Faith

Newton's household also focused on faith. Jackie Newton was the daughter of the founders of Holy Zion Holiness Church, which is now located in Newnan, Georgia. Jackie and her husband have since been appointed in leadership roles at the church. Cecil Newton, who preached his first sermon in 1980, is the pastor at Holy Zion and a bishop for Holy Zion and related congregations. Jackie, who is known as "First Lady Jackie," serves as the praise and worship leader, the director of the women's ministry, and the founder of Mothers And Daughters Excelling (M.A.D.E.), an outreach program providing economic and spiritual support to women and girls.

The message of religion reached their son Cam, who has embraced his faith. Newton has publicly credited God for his success, one time stating, "I thank God every single day. I'm just His instrument, and He's using me on a consistent basis daily. [God is] using me to extend His word, and I'm a prime example of how God could turn something that was bad into something that was very great … If God is with me, who can be against me?"

Newton's parents ensured their sons had well-rounded childhoods outside the church, as well. "We're normal," Cecil Newton said. "We eat out occasionally, we eat at home for the most part. Our values are directly in line with Christian principles and the American mainstream public." Newton was in the Boy Scouts and often known as the class clown. He is the only member of his immediate family who can't play the drums.

Cam Newton was raised in a Christian church, and his faith continues to be important to him.

Cam Newton: Trying to Win Them All

Parental Role Model

More widely known about Newton's parents, and his father in particular, comes down to their role in his football career. Newton's father, Cecil Sr., has received much notoriety in recent years for his role in the recruitment by colleges of his son. However, long before that, Cecil was just a proud dad playing football with his son. He might have been the first to know that Cam was destined to be a quarterback. "We would throw for an hour in the yard," Cecil Newton remembered. "He wouldn't have any arm problems. My other son and other kids, after ten or fifteen minutes, their elbows or shoulders or something were hurting. (Cam) was throwing with such velocity. It would sting your hands, and he never seemed to get tired." For his part, Newton seemed to appreciate the role his father played in his upbringing. When asked by the *Atlanta Journal-Constitution* who his role model was, he said, "My dad, Cecil Newton. He is the person that keeps me straight and gives me guidance."

Newton now is well known for his talent as a football player. But as a child, he seemed too talented to be a one-sport athlete, so he dabbled in several other sports as well. Around age nine, Newton picked up baseball, playing center field. Because of his abilities, Newton also played third base or shortstop at times. Newton's baseball career was short-lived. He said he quit at age fourteen because he was "afraid of the pitches. The kids started getting better and throwing faster, and it would've hurt getting hit by that ball, so I stopped playing."

Not having baseball in his life left a void. Considering his size, Newton thought basketball might be a good fit, so he started playing in the eighth grade. His aggressive athletic spirit ended up being a little too much on the basketball court at times. "I was big and strong, and every time I tried to steal the ball on defense, I'd knock the kid down," Newton wrote for a website. "I had to understand the difference between basketball and football, but it was challenging being so big." Newton ultimately figured out the difference. He was an all-state basketball player during his high school years. However, football was his true passion.

Newton's size was certainly an asset on the football field. His coaches, however, didn't see him as a quarterback in the beginning. His first position was as a **linebacker**, which is a player on defense known for being tough and gritty, making tackles, and chasing after the quarterback. Newton recalls this experience as being pivotal for him developing into the player he became. "It gave me the mechanism to want to hit rather than to cringe at the thought of being hit," he wrote. "So when I got the opportunity to play offense, it was nothing. I wasn't shying away from contact. If anything, I was initiating it. I think that's what kind of made me stand out at an early age. My mom always wondered how I could be afraid of a little baseball when I always had these huge guys chasing me. It's a good question."

Newton attended Westlake High School in Atlanta, Georgia, which is widely known for its football program. In 2005, Westlake had six **alumni** playing in the NFL—more than any other high school in the country. Newton knew he had a lot of work to do to play for this team, so he set out to amaze the high school head coach, Dallas Allen. Newton was successful. Still, playing in such an esteemed program, Newton had to wait his turn.

"I first became aware of Cam when he was a ninth-grader," Allen said. "My JV coach told me, 'We have this kid who I think is going to be pretty good.' I was busy with my season, and I didn't need a third-string quarterback, yada, yada, yada. Then my starter broke

Since he was a youth, Cam Newton has been one of the biggest and most fearless players on his football team.

his finger in practice, and the backup sprained his ankle, and we had to pull him up for a varsity game. I liked his demeanor on the field immediately. He wasn't the player he was going to be. But he was trying to take charge. He had that instinct."

In fact, the first time Newton saw the field was memorable—for the wrong reasons. The game Newton had been called up for was against Westlake's rival, Mays. When the second-string quarterback was hurt, Westlake was close to the end zone and poised to score. Newton's older brother, Cecil Jr., was playing **center**, the person who snaps the ball back to the quarterback. As he always did, Cecil Jr., snapped the ball hard. Newton wasn't ready. The ball bounced on the ground, and Mays recovered the fumble. The Lions ended up losing that game by one point.

After the game, Coach Allen said to the brothers: "You guys live in the same household. Bobbling a snap is the last thing you guys should do." (Cecil Jr., while never achieving the level of athletic fame that Cam has, played four years of college football at Tennessee State.) Still, Allen was impressed at Newton's ability to keep moving forward. "Cam's the kind of kid where things just roll off his back like water," Allen said. "He'd go back in the huddle, ready for the next play." Marquis Slaton, who was then the **offensive coordinator** at Westlake, remembered Newton for the same thing. "He was one of those guys who would not break," Slaton said. "I could chew on his butt and chew on his butt, and he'd just look at me and say, 'Next play, coach.'"

Newton remained the starter for the rest of the season, despite being a work in progress. Being close to those players truly in the spotlight helped motivate Newton. Before he was the one catching anyone's interest, Newton noticed the attention paid to the stars on his high school team. He began getting exposed to the doors that could open for him through athletics. Coaches and scouts from the country's elite conferences and some of the most well-known college teams, such as Georgia Tech, Florida State, Auburn, Florida, University of Southern California, and Texas, showed up at his team's practices and games to recruit some of his older teammates. Newton made sure the bumps in the road didn't get him down; he wanted to be recruited, too.

Working to Improve

To refine his skills, Newton played football as much as he could. Outside of the school team, Newton excelled in the youth football leagues. By age fifteen, Newton was an all-star. The first time he traveled for football was for the seven-on-seven all-star national championship in New York City. Around that time, he started realizing that football could take him places.

Newton has publicly said how important the influence of his head coach was on his development. He also was lucky to have worked under the **tutelage** of Slaton, who can recite Newton's statistics by heart. Slaton was instrumental not only in helping Newton build his game, but also to get him to better understand his role on the field.

Slaton said Newton never had a problem throwing long passes to receivers, but he had more difficulty making the short passes. Newton often threw the ball too hard, making it tough to catch. Slaton worked with him on the field to master his passing, and then he worked off the field with Newton to increase his understanding of the game. Newton once told his coach, "I want to understand the offense the way you do. You have to help me be great." Newton and Slaton started talking two or three times a week for hours after practice, about how to respond to defenses, what footwork to use, how to be a leader and much more. Slaton's mentoring even included how to handle being a public figure in his town. "I needed him to learn right away how to ignore the distractions, people at the grocery store telling him to change how he threw or how great he was, getting in his head," Slaton said.

Newton put himself on the football map with an outstanding junior year in high school. He passed for 2,500 yards and 23 touchdowns that season. He also ran for 638 yards and 9 touchdowns. Rivals.com, a popular website that ranks college prospects, listed Newton as a **five-star prospect** and the number-two quarterback in the country that year.

Several games during Newton's career were particularly memorable. Statesboro High School had been undefeated at home for three straight seasons when Newton and Westlake entered its stadium. Newton was held out for the first half, and his team fell behind. During the second half, he led the offense to 51 points and a huge win.

In October 2006, Westlake had lost three games in a row, all in the final seconds. Newton helped his team bounce back with a 42-3 win over Woodward Academy, in which he had a hand in five touchdowns—he ran for three and threw for two.

One of the parts of his game that made Newton so attractive to colleges was his status as a "**dual-threat**" quarterback. This meant that while Newton could throw the ball well, he also could be trusted to run with the ball. Knowing Newton could be successful in both ways made defending him extremely challenging. Coach Allen said: "When you look at some of the quarterbacks in the state, they are athletes that play quarterback. In Cameron's case, he is a quarterback who happens to be an athlete." Allen also knew that college coaches were interested in Newton because of how difficult it was for defenders to take down Newton even if they could catch him. "They tackled him by jumping on his back or tripping him up," Allen said. "He was as big as most defensive linemen and bigger than most linebackers."

Big Body and Personality

Newton's size was beneficial on the basketball court at the high school level, as well. His high-school basketball coach, Darron Rogers, said, "He could work from the wing, he could post you up and dunk on you, and he could have gone to Division I college ball if he had wanted." In its annual preview section, the *Atlanta Journal-Constitution* highlighted Newton, saying: "The 6-6, 230-pounder has the finesse to be an all-state quarterback, but is also rugged enough to be a power forward on the basketball court."

In addition to being an incredible athlete, Newton also was known as a big personality. For example, in a varsity basketball team picture, he sits among seventeen teammates, most with the scowl that teenage boys so typically wear when they're being photographed. Newton, however, is grinning from ear to ear. Milton Robinson, a maintenance worker at Newton's former high school, said the person everyone is seeing on national TV these days represents the same boy he knew years ago. "The way Cam is, all smiling and enjoying himself, that's how he was when I got to know him. I was talking with him last week, and I'm telling him, 'You're still the same as you were as a freshman,' and he's coming back at me with, 'I guess it's too late to change now; it's who I am.'"

Cam Newton's college announcement was a big deal. Fans of the University of Florida were thrilled when he chose to play for the Gators.

Cam Newton: Trying to Win Them All

Allen, Newton's football coach, remembered Newton coordinating a giant prank on senior day: Newton and his upper-class teammates threw loads of water balloons at the underclassmen. But this off-the-field fun wasn't seen as a distraction to Newton. These hijinks were just part of who he is as a person.

College football teams are certainly interested in what kind of person they are recruiting. But, to those interested in having Newton on their team, the smile and joking nature were secondary. College coaches wanted Newton because they thought he would help them win. ESPN's scouting report on Newton called him "a monster of an athlete and huge pocket passer with deceptive speed and quickness. He looks like an athletic receiving tight end. Essentially we would describe him as a pocket passer with the ability to get out of trouble and make some plays with his legs."

On September 8, 2006, Cam Newton held a press conference to announce his college decision. After noting all the people in his life to whom he owed his success, the time came for Newton to announce what his next step would be. He said: "I am overwhelmed with all the scholarship offers I have received. Unfortunately, I can only attend one university, even though I would like to attend all of them. It was a tough decision, determined with much thought, research, and prayer. My commitment can only be to one school. With that said, the university I will be attending after graduating is the University of Florida."

Crazily enough, only three college programs had recruited Newton as a quarterback. Other teams were interested in him as a tight end or a defensive back. Before committing to Florida, Newton entertained scholarship offers from Georgia, Maryland, University of Mississippi, Mississippi State, Oklahoma, and

Virginia Tech. The Florida recruiter in charge of bringing Newton to Gainesville was Stan Drayton, a former NFL running backs coach who was hired by the University of Texas in 2017 to be its running game coordinator. In 2007, Drayton was named one of the nation's top recruiters by Rivals.com, in part because of his ability to lure Newton to the Florida program.

Newton left his mark on an already well-known high-school football program. Everyone expected he would be making a splash at the next level.

Chapter 2

Growing Pains

In Glendale, Arizona, on January 8, 2007, the University of Florida football team beat Ohio State to win the Bowl Championship Series (BCS) National Championship. Months later, the University of Florida men's basketball team won the national championship — the first time a school won both titles in the same school year. Gator Nation, as the fans were called, was riding high and had high hopes the school would maintain its place on top of the **collegiate** sports world. Would Cam Newton be the one to help them stay there? That was his plan.

Cam Newton stepped foot on campus in Gainesville, Florida in the fall of 2007 as the headlining recruit for a very strong class of newcomers. He arrived to much fanfare, with coaches and teammates expecting big things from him down the line. The problem was: Cam Newton would have to wait his turn.

When Newton arrived in Gainesville, the quarterback leading the team was Tim Tebow, then a sophomore. Tebow was known for his straitlaced lifestyle, his strict adherence to his Christian faith,

Opposite: Tim Tebow (*right*) was the starting quarterback at the University of Florida when Cam Newton arrived in the fall of 2007.

and his ability to scramble with the football. Newton, meanwhile, brought his same personality and charm from high school with him to Florida.

Newton's teammates had several different takes on him. Many saw his potential, including Cornelius Ingram, who said, "We thought the program would be in good hands for a long time with him. You could see [the ability] when he got in the game." Teammate Markihe Anderson noted Newton had "some goofiness to him." However, several unnamed teammates said that because Newton knew Tebow was the unquestioned starter, it caused Newton to lose focus at practice. "He wasn't always putting his best foot forward [as a backup]," former Gators running back Brandon James said. "Guys would always speak to him, remind him to take things seriously —'You're going to be special.'"

The Florida Gators did not have the same success in the 2007 season that they had had the year before, when the team won thirteen of fourteen games. During the 2007 regular season, Florida won nine games and lost three times. They won five of eight games in the Southeastern Conference (SEC), the **preeminent** football conference. On New Year's Day, Florida played the University of Michigan in the Capital One Bowl and lost, 41-35. However, Tim Tebow's performance was a highlight throughout the season. Tebow became the first college sophomore to win the Heisman Trophy, which is awarded by New York's Downtown Athletic Club to college football's most outstanding player at the end of each season. Tebow set a school record for the number of rushing yards by a quarterback in a single game. He also set SEC records for the number of rushing touchdowns for a quarterback during a season and the total number of touchdowns (thirty-two passing and twenty-three rushing) for a quarterback during any season. Tebow also had one game in which he scored five touchdowns.

Newton, meanwhile, made appearances in only five games and totaled forty yards passing, 103 yards rushing, and three touchdowns for the whole season.

Run of Misfortune

However, if Cam Newton saw his opportunity to take over the program dwindling, he didn't tell anyone. In fact, despite Tebow's monster season, it seemed as if Newton might get his chance to leave more of a mark. Prior to the Gators' game against Michigan, Florida coach Urban Meyer voiced his interest in having another quarterback share the load with Tebow. The main reason Meyer had for this plan was to protect Tebow's health; Tebow had experienced a broken hand and an injured right non-throwing shoulder during his Heisman season. Meyer said: "Next year, we'll play two quarterbacks for sure. We'll have to. I don't think (Tebow) can stand three years of that punishment. We'll have to be smart."

In the following offseason, Newton received mixed reviews, with particular concern for his ability to pass accurately. Still, Newton had proved himself enough to make his way onto the field in the opening game of the 2008 season. Unfortunately for Newton, he injured his ankle and was taken out of the game. Newton had passed for fourteen yards and rushed for ten yards and a touchdown. Though Newton didn't know it at the time, his season was over. Compounding his ankle injury, in early November Newton injured his neck in a car accident. Newton chose to take a "medical redshirt" for the year, meaning he decided he would sit out the whole year because he anticipated the injury would sideline him for at least a significant part of it. This would then allow him to extend his college playing career. (Newton ultimately had reparative surgery in 2014 to tighten the ankle ligaments and give him more range of motion.) The rest of Newton's story may have been completely different had this injury never happened.

With Newton on the bench, Tebow again rose to the occasion. The Gators finished the season with a 13-1 record and a 24-14 victory over Oklahoma on January 8, 2009, in the BCS National Championship Game.

However, Newton wasn't there to enjoy the win. On November 21, 2008, Newton had been arrested for reportedly stealing another student's laptop computer, which had been painted with a forest scene to distinguish it from others. Newton was charged with felony counts of burglary, larceny, and obstructing justice.

The investigation into Newton also was unfavorable. A fellow student at Florida reported having his laptop stolen on October 16, 2008. The laptop was linked to Newton five days later when the username "cnewton" logged on to access the school's network. When investigators went to Newton's dormitory, they noticed a laptop that had been painted black and had "Cam Newton" written on top in white paint. While police checked to see if the serial numbers matched, Newton asked for privacy to speak to his attorney. During that time, Newton reportedly threw the laptop out his window, to dispose of the evidence. The computer was later found in a trash bin outside the dorm; the police report said, "Mr. Newton threw the computer out of his window." Newton was held in Alachua County Jail for two days that he later said "felt like four years. Everything that I valued in my life was taken away."

While at the University of Florida, Cam Newton was arrested for stealing a laptop that belonged to a fellow student.

Newton was suspended from the football team. While charges against Newton were ultimately dropped after he completed a pre-trial intervention program for first-time offenders, he was beginning to feel like Florida might not be the place for him to make a name for himself. He agreed to complete 180 hours of community service at his former high school. At the end of the Fall 2008 semester, Newton announced he would transfer from Florida.

Years later, Newton reflected on the mistakes he made.

When I was at the University of Florida, it was at a time in my life where I was childish. I didn't communicate with my family on a regular basis. I really would put entertainment before my family, my roots.

I was so disconnected from the reality of what my purpose was. I did things that I didn't think about doing. I just did it without thinking about the repercussions from it.

When I didn't have my scholarship [any] more, I was empty. It was like I did a whole 180, and instead of being that guy that people was like, 'Be like Cam,' it was, 'Man, don't be like Cam. Look at him: he's back here now, taking out trash, cleaning boards, filing papers.'

If you look at my life, it's obvious things that I've done I regret. Looking back at it, it's like, 'Dang! How stupid could you be?' It was kind of like I hit the reset button. OK, now I've got to learn from this, and I'm going to be better from it.

Getting Out of Tebow's Shadow

At the time of his announcement, Newton gave another reason for the scheduled departure. Newton stated he was transferring due to the fact that Tim Tebow decided he was going to return to Florida for his senior year, rather than enter the NFL draft. "I think I was left with no choice but to leave," Newton said. "I felt like if [Tebow] comes back for his senior year, I really wasn't going to get a chance to play, and that was another year washed down the drain." Newton wasn't interested in being a backup any longer.

In subsequent years, reports surfaced that point to another possible reason why Newton chose to leave the Florida program after the fall semester in 2008. Newton was being accused of three instances of academic cheating, one in his freshman year and two in his sophomore year. During his sophomore year, he was reported to have been caught putting his name on another student's paper and buying a replacement paper online. The report states that Newton would have faced expulsion or suspension if he were found guilty. Newton dodged these allegations during a press conference while he was at Auburn in November 2010. "I don't want to beat a dead horse talking about it," he said. "It's not going to affect me. Am I hurt? No. Am I curious? A little bit. … There's a lot of speculations, rumors going around. I'm not going to be up here entertaining them. I'm a person who came a long way. Would I change it? No. That's how I matured as a person and as a player. I'm continuously trying to learn about this crazy thing called life. It would be selfish of me to entertain anything said about me. That's pretty much it."

For whatever reason Newton actually left Florida—the injuries, the laptop theft, the threat of expulsion, or Tebow's continued presence on the team—the next step he took was the beginning of his next chapter. Newton announced he would be transferring to Blinn College in Brenham, Texas, just days before Florida played in the championship game. From a life in the limelight, Newton's next step would be anything but. "I believe it was all calculated," said Jeff Tilley, Blinn's marketing and communications director. "If you want to pick somewhere that's secluded, to get away from the limelight, to take care of business, I can't think of a more perfect place. You could tell that Cam understood. This was his last chance to get back on track."

Blinn, a two-year college about 75 miles (120 kilometers) northwest of Houston, presented many things Newton was unaccustomed to. First: the cows. Newton's 100-square-foot (9.2 square meter) dorm room was adjacent to a cow pasture. The mooing often woke him up at night. The glitz and glam of a high-profile university also was nowhere to be found. Newton's dorm room didn't have a TV, and he took his classes in a brick structure called "The Classroom Building," which was the same place his coach's office was located. Newton's team "gear" was limited to one school logo T-shirt, one pair of shoes, and one pair of socks — all of which he was expected to wash on his own. Downtown Brenham had a homemade pie shop, antique stores, and two bars, one of which doubled as a produce stand. Gainesville, this was not.

Chance to Play

However, Blinn also provided Newton with something that had been lacking in Florida: the chance to play. If Newton was focused on distancing himself from his past, he needed to land at a place where he could propel himself to a brighter future. Blinn coach Brad Franchione remembered how meticulous Newton and his family were with this decision. "There were some questions," Franchione said. "Obviously Cam is a physical presence and [his family] wanted to know that we were going to work on his progress as a passer— a pocket passer, a play-action passer—as opposed to just running the option. They didn't want to come to Blinn if we were just going to use him as an option quarterback to try to win games and let him run over everybody."

Franchione admits that he and his staff did their own investigation into Newton, too, to make sure that the ghosts of Newton's past wouldn't follow him to Blinn. They were assured by the coaching and the academic staff at Florida that he was both a student and a player in good standing. Both parties knew this commitment would last one football season, as Newton hoped success at Blinn would springboard him back into the big leagues. Newton showed up in Brenham, a town of about sixteen thousand residents, with only a Nike duffel bag. He slept on his coach's couch the first night in town. He and the coaches had an agreement that he would follow a three-step plan: Get a degree; become a better leader; continue his growth as a football player. Each of those three areas took Franchione's commitment and Newton's focus.

On the football field, Blinn quickly realized it had a star in the making. In the team's fourth game of the season, against conference rival Tyler Junior College, Newton himself accounted for 503 of Blinn's 601 total yards and more than half of his team's 50 points. In a game later that season, he scored seven touchdowns. In total, Newton passed for 2,833 yards, rushed for 655, and accounted for 39 total touchdowns in twelve games.

Lessons in Leadership

One might argue that Cam Newton's greatest strength as a young quarterback was his ability and desire to lean on those around him to guide him in his development. In the same way he picked the brain of his high school offensive coordinator, Newton expected Blinn College head coach Brad Franchione to give him the keys to the next level. Newton's father expected the same: During a dinner with Franchione, before Cam committed to play for Blinn, Cecil Newton

Coach Brad Franchione helped Cam Newton develop as a player and a leader at Blinn College. Here he celebrates winning a national title.

made the coach promise he would help his son develop as a leader.

The arrangement was simple, in theory. Newton and Franchione would meet every day. Around 11:00 a.m., Newton would stop by his coach's office, asking for his daily motivation. However, Newton wanted real lessons that would springboard him to the next level; he didn't want just run-of-the-mill mantras. Franchione said he would lose sleep combing through books on leadership to quench Newton's thirst for his "lesson of the day." He assigned Newton to read *Leadership is an Art* by Max De Pree, which Newton then carried everywhere.

Franchione remembered feeling as if it was his duty to meet Newton's expectations. "If I didn't have something prepared for him, he was real quick to let me know, 'Yeah, coach. Today's ... wasn't very good,'" Franchione recalled. "'You're going to have to come back with something better tomorrow.'" Franchione was up to the task, and Newton put those lessons into action.

Newton's on-field performance was perhaps secondary to the growth Newton showed as a leader. The commitment Newton's Gator teammates saw lacking was front and center at Blinn. Newton's teammates saw him as an extension of the head coach, firing up the offense on every play in practice. He was the first to arrive and, even during the season's first practice, he stayed forty-five minutes longer to get in extra repetitions. Over the next month, his wide receivers began to follow his lead, not wanting to disappoint their quarterback.

Finding Time for Fun

Newton's personality came with him, of course. Newton once choreographed a celebration dance with his wide receivers in which the group of them huddled in the end zone then dropped to the ground in sync. On another occasion, Newton swiped a penalty flag from a referee's

Blinn College won the National Junior College Athletic Association national championship during Cam Newton's one year on campus.

pocket and threw it in the air to celebrate a win, while his opponents and the referees were left confused. He didn't save all his antics for game day. After a practice during the week before Blinn was playing a lackluster opponent, Newton created a rap to keep his teammates motivated. The video of his rap has been viewed almost 1.4 million times on YouTube.

Newton's brand of mixing work with play translated to success for Blinn. The college won the National Junior College Athletic Association national championship during Newton's only year on campus. "That competitive spirit kind of fueled the team, and I always attributed the national championship with what we were able to accomplish with that group of kids to the competitive spirit that Cam brought," Coach Franchione said. "He fed the monster, and the monster just grew."

Newton also accomplished his academic goal, earning his associate's degree. He was remembered particularly by his English teacher for never being absent or late and engaging in every class discussion. She said he was quiet and respectful, as she recalled the name of Newton's semester-long research paper: "The Life of the Student Athlete."

That life had led Newton from his hometown in College Park, Georgia, to Gainesville, Florida to Brenham, Texas. As he had planned, Newton's journey would not end there. Before moving on, though, Newton reflected on his time at Blinn, calling it a "humbling experience." He knew he had it in him to be a big-time quarterback, but he wasn't playing on a big-time stage for a whole year of his college career. "I go from the University of Florida, where I can get Gatorade at my beck and call, to a place where you have to help paint your stadium stands," he said. "I have no regrets about the road I

Cam Newton: Trying to Win Them All

took. The only regret I have is that people stereotype my situation as a negative situation. As an athlete, you have to take the good with the bad. I learned a lot during my tenure at Florida. I wouldn't say it was a waste. Everybody's road's going to be different."

As the time to choose a four-year school—again—came nearer, six schools had officially made offers to Newton: Auburn, Arizona, Mississippi State, Oklahoma, Kansas State, and North Carolina. Between September and December of 2009, Newton visited four of those schools. Before the New Year's Eve ball would drop, Newton's next destination would be announced.

3

Season of Firsts

O n New Year's Eve 2009, Cam Newton announced to the football-watching world that his journey would continue at Auburn University in Auburn, Alabama. This decision meant Newton would be returning to the Southeastern Conference, widely considered to be the top tier of collegiate competition. Newton had been headlined as the number-one junior-college transfer, and Auburn fans were truly excited he would become a Tiger. One well-known Auburn fan blog announced Newton's decision with this headline: "Cameron Newton Commits, Commence Drooling."

Auburn's Sports Information/Media Relations Director, Kirk Sampson, had written the original press release, to inform the media outlets of Newton's pending arrival, but even he didn't know the impact this one player would have on the school. It became obvious quickly that Newton had the "it" factor—a special quality that drew others to him. "He was a quarterback in a defensive end's body,

Opposite: Fans of Auburn University celebrated Cam Newton's arrival from Blinn College.

had a great personality and a smile that would light up a room," Sampson remembered.

Newton set out to make an impression on the field from the first day. Coaches at Auburn remember him, after his arrival in January 2010, frequently arising at 7:00 a.m. just to get in throwing sessions on cold Saturday mornings. Despite all the excitement that came with Newton's arrival in Auburn, he encountered a familiar circumstance: having to compete for the starting quarterback job. He worked extra hard throughout the winter and spring to ensure he would be the starter.

Newton had said he was drawn originally to Auburn's family-like atmosphere. In April, he officially became the head of the household. Auburn coach Gene Chizik announced in a statement that Newton would be their leader: "After thoroughly evaluating our quarterbacks during spring practice and over the last week, Cam has emerged as our post-spring No. 1 quarterback. Obviously, he will have a lot of work to do over the summer and during two-a-days to continue along this path. We fully expect our other quarterbacks to continue to work hard and compete with Cam during the offseason and into fall camp." The other quarterbacks may have continued to compete with Newton, but he never came close to losing his role on top.

Good First Impression

It didn't take Newton much time on the field to sell everyone on the idea that he was a star. During week one of the 2010 college football season, Newton's Tigers hosted Arkansas State. Newton's passing game was good; he completed nine of fourteen pass attempts for a total of 186 yards and three touchdowns. However, Newton's

Cam Newton: Trying to Win Them All

ability to be a running quarterback is what really became clear. He rushed for 171 yards and two touchdowns—including one of 71 yards. After his first game back playing for a major college football powerhouse, he was named the SEC Offensive Player of the Week.

Several weeks later, Newton had an incredible game against South Carolina: he passed for two touchdowns in addition to rushing for 176 yards and three touchdowns. He also had a touchdown run, on which he leaped over the line from the 1, nullified by a penalty. One of the rushing touchdowns came in the first quarter to open the scoring. On first down, Newton took off down the right sideline and dived into the end zone to compete a 54-yard run. The crowd erupted in cheers. Commentators and football experts began wondering if Newton would be in the discussion for the Heisman Trophy. Then, on October 9, 2010, Newton ran for 132 yards and four touchdowns on the road against the University of Kentucky—all in the first half. When Kentucky rallied to tie the game in the fourth quarter, Newton led Auburn on a long drive that ended with the game-winning field goal. Newton finished with 198 yards rushing and 210 passing. Everyone was abuzz.

Newton had solidified his place in the Heisman conversation. Auburn had been home to two previous Heisman Trophy winners: quarterback Pat Sullivan and running back Bo Jackson. It was looking more and more like Newton might be the third.

Meanwhile, he wasn't the only one having success. His team also remained undefeated.

Against Arkansas, Newton had another "Heisman moment," bowling over an opposing linebacker on his way to the end zone. Then, against Louisiana State University, Newton outran an All-American safety en route to a touchdown. By then it was late

Cam Newton first showed his "Super Man" abilities scoring a touchdown on a 54-yard run against South Carolina in 2010.

Cam Newton: Trying to Win Them All

October, and Auburn got serious about starting Newton's Heisman campaign—though it didn't take much work. In the 24/7 news cycle of Facebook, Twitter, YouTube, and the SEC television station, anyone paying attention knew about the prowess of Cam Newton— for better or worse. "There were no more scooter rides around campus, no walking into a public place without being noticed," recalled Sampson, the sports information director. "Through all the rising fame, Cam never changed, but the world around him did."

Pay-to-Play Allegations

Newton's on-field success did not stall throughout the season, but outside distractions again arose. In early November, several reputable media outlets reported that Newton was the focus of an investigation being undertaken by the National Collegiate Athletic Association (NCAA). A man who said he represented Newton allegedly was soliciting almost $200,000 from schools that wanted Newton to transfer to their team from Blinn (prior to Newton committing to Auburn). College athletes are not allowed to be paid for their participation on sports teams. Newton, put simply, was being accused of not following the rules by trying to make money while still playing college football.

ESPN reported that a former Mississippi State football player and current sports agent named Kenny Rogers claimed to be "representing" Newton in his process of deciding which school he would attend after finishing junior college. Rogers was reported to have contacted a former teammate, John Bond, saying "It would take some cash to get Cam" to come to Mississippi State. Bond said he was told that other schools were offering Newton $200,000 to play for them, but since Newton really liked Mississippi State, he would accept $180,000. Bond reported this outreach to the Mississippi State athletic director, who contacted the Southeastern Conference. (In addition to athletes getting in trouble for soliciting money from schools, the schools themselves can also get in trouble for offering money to athletes.)

Defending his actions, Bond said: "I have no agenda other than protecting Mississippi State. We've done what we were supposed to do from the very beginning. Mississippi State has done nothing wrong, and I've done nothing wrong. It's been handed off to the NCAA, and it's in their hands now. I don't know what happened at Auburn. I don't know why he went to Auburn. That's not my concern."

When this news came out, Newton faced a firestorm of accusations and questions. Most of all, many people wondered if the investigation might jeopardize Newton's **eligibility** to play for the rest of the season.

Newton's father, Cecil Newton, became a prime target of the investigation. The NCAA came to believe that Cecil had been instrumental in orchestrating the financial exchange. Cecil Newton, when the report was initiated, said: "If Rogers tried to solicit money from Mississippi State, he did it on his own, without our knowledge."

Cam Newton's family's business also was checked out. Cecil Newton is the pastor of the Holy Zion Center of Deliverance in Newnan, Georgia, and he was asked by the NCAA to provide financial documents as part of its investigation. The church had been in the news in recent years as it was in danger of being demolished for failing to meet the city's building code. Finally, those renovations were under way and the church was able to stay open, leading some to wonder where the funds came from. Still, Jackie Newton, Cam's

The Holy Zion Center of Deliverance church building in Newnan, Georgia, is not a glamorous facility that is worth a lot of money.

mother, said the church is not glamorous. "If you've ever seen our church, you'd know we don't have any money," she said. "We have nothing."

Highs and Lows

The end of November was a frantic time: on November 26, 2010, Newton led a second-half comeback as Auburn beat rival Alabama, 28-27. On November 28, Auburn returned to the number-one spot in the Bowl Championship Series (BCS) rankings, which determines which teams compete for the national championship. On November 29, Newton was named the SEC offensive player of the week for the sixth time that season. That same day, the NCAA declared "a violation of **amateurism** rules occurred."

Then on November 30, 2010—just four days before the

Southeastern Conference championship game—Auburn made a decision based on the NCAA's findings: Cam Newton was declared ineligible. He could not play for the conference championship or (potentially) the national championship, and he would be out of the running for the Heisman Trophy. Newton was found to be guilty of violating NCAA Bylaw 12.3.3, which states: "Any individual, agency or organization that represents a prospective student-athlete for compensation in placing the prospect in a collegiate institution as a recipient of institutional financial aid shall be considered an agent or organization marketing the individual's athletics ability or reputation." The NCAA claimed that Kenny Rogers was acting as Newton's agent, trying to solicit money in order for Newton to play for a certain school.

However, the suspension did not last for long. Less than a day later, Newton was **reinstated**. The NCAA found that Cecil Newton, in contradiction to his earlier statements, was in fact seeking money for his son to attend Mississippi State in what was termed a "pay-for-play scenario." However, Cam Newton himself could not be held responsible.

Kevin Lennon, the NCAA vice president for academic and membership affairs, explained the decision: "In determining how a violation impacts a student-athlete's eligibility, we must consider the young person's responsibility. Based on the information available to the reinstatement staff at this time, we do not have sufficient evidence that Cam Newton or anyone from Auburn was aware of this activity, which led to his reinstatement." Put simply: Newton's father was breaking the rules, but since Newton didn't know, he couldn't be punished. The NCAA further said that Auburn "limited" the access that Cecil Newton had to the Auburn football program.

Years later, Cecil Newton said he "willfully fell on the sword" to take the focus off his son. He also denied his role being as extreme as the investigation found. Cecil Newton said, "There was one individual who tried to navigate services for Cam. Were we promised stuff? Were we gifted with stuff of this sort? No. Never. No one took money."

All this took place during the week Newton was trying to prepare for a game that, if won, would take his team to the national championship. To watch the game, one would not have known about all this turbulence going on behind the scenes. Auburn beat South Carolina, 56-17, and secured its spot in the national championship game. Newton threw four touchdown passes and ran for two more, becoming just the third quarterback in NCAA history to both run and throw for twenty touchdowns in a single season. Newton's 408 yards of total offense were the second most ever by a player in the SEC Championship Game.

Auburn's Chizik marveled over the athletic phenomenon that Cam Newton had become:

> If you look over a thirteen-game span, I've never seen anything like it, to be honest with you. It's running the ball. It's throwing the ball. Usually great quarterbacks do one or the other better. I think what God's blessed Cameron with is the ability to do both really, really well. He's probably the best football player I've ever seen.

Newton, who had been with this team for only one season, was carried off the field on the shoulders of the offensive linemen; four of the starters on the line were seniors. Newton's coaches marveled over the impact Newton had on this team in just eleven months. "For a guy to come in and only be around one year and develop those kinds of relationships and that kind of leadership ability, I think that speaks volumes about Cam Newton," Auburn defensive coordinator Ted Roof recalled. "Maybe the most veteran offensive line in the country: They showed how much they respected him. You can't manufacture that. That's real." Newton himself said the moment was touching: "When they told me they wanted to put me on their shoulders, I thought it was a joke at first," he said. "But as I went up in the air, it hit a part of my heart that I will never take away."

In the Heisman Spotlight

The spotlight would only grow brighter for Newton. Seven days after leading his team to a win in the SEC Championship game, Newton was in New York City at the Best Buy Theater in Times Square for the Heisman Trophy ceremony. The other **nominees** were quarterback Andrew Luck of Stanford, running back LaMichael James of Oregon, and quarterback Kellen Moore of Boise State. Almost everyone knew ahead of time that Newton was a sure thing to win, and it only became clearer that most of the world knew who Newton was. Kirk Sampson, the sports information director for Auburn, remembered the autograph hounds at every corner and random passers-by reaching out to the quarterback. "As we walked across 45th Street to the Best Buy Theatre for the Heisman ceremony and one of the most impressive Tiger Walks ever (Auburn players walk to their stadium for games between two lines of fans), a New Yorker in a delivery truck stuck his head out the window and yelled, 'Yo Cam, congrats!'" Sampson recalled. "It wasn't the first or last time during the Heisman weekend that people greeted Cam or

Despite being at Auburn for only one season, Cam Newton was looked up to by his teammates, who carried him off the field after the SEC title game.

Cam Newton: Trying to Win Them All

took pictures, but it was that delivery driver that made me come to the realization that Cam had achieved rock-star status."

If he was a star *before* the ceremony, his status was only solidified during it. As is the tradition at the Heisman Trophy presentation, as many of the past winners as possible are on stage to greet the new member of their community of college football stars. The nominees were reminded by the emcee that "The gentlemen standing behind me (the past winners) are ready to welcome one of you into the elite Heisman fraternity. From now on, your name will always be followed by 'Heisman Trophy winner.'"

As predicted, Newton was the winner of college football's most prized individual honor. When his name was announced, Newton ducked his head down into his hands, grinning with the smile he had long been known for. Newton won in a landslide, receiving 729 first-place votes. Luck, the runner-up, received 78 first-place votes. On his way to accepting the award, Newton shook hands with the other nominees and then walked over to his mother and wrapped her in a long embrace. "When I reached my mother I really didn't want to let go," Newton said. "It's been hard for me, but it's been extremely hard for her just to see how much her son has been through and I just wanted to hug her the whole night to make her feel at ease." Newton's father was not present, having issued a statement earlier in the week that he did not want to "rob Cam and the event of a sacred moment."

Despite the fact that Newton was widely expected to win, he needed a moment to steady himself before giving his acceptance speech. He even whispered "Oh my God" to himself before pulling his speech out of his jacket pocket. While at the lectern, Newton thanked God, his mother, his father, his coaches, his family, his

Cam Newton was awarded the 2010 Heisman Trophy, which is given each season to college football's most outstanding player.

teammates, his school's president, the Heisman trustees and the troops overseas. He spoke to the support he so appreciated, seemingly talking directly to his mom at one point:

> My parents do a lot of things behind the scenes that go unnoticed. This is not an award, in my opinion, that has been won in my play this year. This is an award that's been won ever since I came out of your womb. Thank you for everything that you do for me. … And to my father, I love you so much. It's amazing what God can do in a person's life. Who would ever have thought a person from College Park, Georgia would get an award with such prestige and tradition? I thank God every single day for waking me up this morning and giving me the ability to play the great game of football.

Newton's college football journey had one more stop: Glendale, Arizona, home to the BCS National Championship Game on January 10, 2011. Newton's Tigers, who were favored slightly, played against Heisman contender LaMichael James and the Oregon Ducks. The game was back-and-forth and hard-fought. Newton directed a final drive that ended with a field goal as time expired to give Auburn a 22-19 victory.

With the win, Auburn had earned its first national championship since 1957, capping a perfect 14-0 season that was once considered improbable. "I guarantee you five or six months ago, nobody would have bet their last dollar to say that Auburn University is winning the national championship," Newton said. "And now … we're smiling right now."

The game was Newton's last at the college level. In his one season at Auburn, Newton rushed for 1,473 yards and twenty touchdowns and passed for 2,854 yards and thirty touchdowns. On January 13, 2011—three days after the national championship game—he issued a statement that he would be declaring for the National Football League (NFL) draft. "This decision was difficult for me and my family," Newton said in his statement. "It's been a blessing for me to be a part of something so great. Any time you win games it's a big deal, but for this school to win a BCS national championship, what a way to make people happy. Auburn is a special place that I can call home."

Immediately, Newton was analyzed by NFL draft experts, most of whom were very impressed. Scouting profiles called Newton "one of the most athletically gifted quarterbacks in draft history," "nothing but unbelievable," "the most naturally talented player in the 2011 draft," and "From his overall body mass to his length, there's simply not many quarterbacks like him on the planet." Newton was known for his athleticism and his deceptive quickness. There were questions raised about his accuracy with long passes. Some scouts also thought Newton needed to develop more "field vision," knowing he would be facing defenses more complex in the NFL than he had while in college.

Others questioned his decision-making ability—not on the field, but off of it, given his involvement in scandals at Florida and while at Auburn. Leading up to the draft, some experts wondered if Blaine Gabbert, then the quarterback at Missouri, would be chosen over Newton. Gabbert hadn't been involved in any off-the-field issues; in addition to being talented, maybe Gabbert would be a safer pick, some thought. The Carolina Panthers had the first pick

Tough to the Finish

Cam Newton and the Auburn Tigers faced their fair share of difficult games throughout the 2010 regular season. Six of their twelve regular-season games were won by eight or fewer points. The biggest test came on the biggest stage. Following a series of weeks during which outside scandal seemed poised to rock the Tigers off their course, Newton and his teammates squared off against the Oregon Ducks at the University of Phoenix Stadium in Glendale, Arizona.

ESPN called the game a "bruising battle." Oregon had been averaging a nation-leading forty-nine points per game. Auburn was led by the Heisman Trophy

Cam Newton and the Auburn Tigers won the national championship in January 2011 against the Oregon Ducks in a "bruising battle."

winner. Both teams were known for having dynamic and high-powered offenses, so many expected the game to be high scoring. In fact, the two teams amassed their second-lowest point totals for the 2010 season in a gritty, back-and-forth contest. Auburn had to overcome deficits several times throughout the game and leaned more on running back Michael Dyer, the game's Most Valuable Player, than anyone. Dyer carried the ball twenty-two times and gained 143 yards. Thirty-seven of those yards came on one carry on the game's final drive. Newton also carried twenty-two times, but was limited to 64 yards.

Newton did what he had to do, completing twenty of thirty-four passes and throwing for two touchdowns with one interception. Newton also took a big hit in the fourth quarter from which he was slow to get up. Still he stayed in the game and completed the 73-yard drive that took Auburn to the Oregon 2-yard line. At the end of it all, Auburn was the victor, winning, 22—19, on a 19-yard field goal. While his teammates celebrated, Newton was getting X-rays to make sure nothing was broken. He would turn out to be fine. Asked how he felt by a reporter, Newton said, "It was worth it."

in the draft, and they were widely known to be interested in drafting a quarterback.

Draft Disagreements

Draft experts knew that some teams might be scared off by Newton and the stream of scandal that had seemed to follow him to this point in his career. However, they were wowed by his play. Mel Kiper of ESPN said "I had Newton going No. 1 in my mock draft. He had so much more talent than anyone else. He was like Superman—if you could just square away the **intangibles**." Adam Schefter of ESPN, one of the most reliable sports reporters in the business, wavered between his predictions about the draft, calling Newton "about as polarizing a figure as there could be for an eventual No. 1 pick."

The Panthers' owner, Jerry Richardson, was known for being conservative, and many wondered if Newton's style might clash with Richardson's view of what a quarterback should look and act like. Warren Moon, a Hall of Fame quarterback who served as a mentor to Newton, shared his observation: "Cam is a little bit outgoing, and he had some history—things he went through in college. Mr. Richardson had to swallow that and digest it. Remember: he (Richardson) said he didn't want a QB that had cornrows, tattoos all over … This was going to be a sell job."

NFL teams are always diligent with getting to know the players they may draft and ultimately pay millions and millions of dollars. With Newton, the process was no different. Marty Hurney, the Panthers' general manager, and Ron Rivera, the Panthers' newly

Opposite: NFL Commissioner Roger Goodell (*left*) announced the Carolina Panthers chose Cam Newton with the first overall pick of the 2011 National Football League draft.

hired head coach, met with Newton for four hours near Auburn. They wanted to get to the root of things. Newton, it turned out, was a good salesperson. Hurney walked away from the meeting with positive thoughts about Newton. "The more research we did, as we talked to everybody, they all said the same thing: Cam was dedicated, had a great work ethic," said Hurney, a former sportswriter. "A lot of the things written about him we didn't find to be true. From that process, it just felt like he was our guy."

The Panthers, however, made Newton no promises. Leading up to the draft on April 28, 2011, Newton wasn't sure which team would select him or when. Rivera later said the Panthers didn't hesitate. Commissioner Roger Goodell walked across the stage and announced: "With the first pick in the 2011 NFL draft, the Carolina Panthers select Cam Newton, quarterback, Auburn." Newton flashed his trademark grin, celebrated with family, and walked toward the stage to put on the blue Carolina baseball cap and pose with the commissioner for a photo.

Chris Berman, one of the ESPN commentators covering the draft, remarked again at Newton's unique physical skills, saying, "Hope springs eternal in the NFL draft, and Cam Newton is a specimen unlike most any others ever to play the position."

Many news organizations debated the difference between Newton and Gabbert, a discussion that looks ridiculous in hindsight as Gabbert has struggled as a pro. Rivera has remembered in recent years how difficult the decision was between the two:

> Those were the two guys we targeted and looked at, and looked at really, really hard. What gave Newton the final edge had something to do with the scandal in which he was embroiled—and the fact that he came

through it successfully. … It's one of those things as you go through it, you look for certain things, certain characteristics, and probably the biggest thing that was different was the situation Cam had been in—going through the adversity and then coming out on top. Cam was tremendously impressive.

With the draft, Newton continued to set records. He had become the first quarterback in the modern era to win the Heisman Trophy, win the national championship, and become the first overall pick in the NFL draft.

Chapter 4

Professional Growth

Every **rookie** quarterback in the NFL is kept under a microscope. Football fans everywhere want to know: Will he be any good? Will his success playing college football translate to the professional game? Will the pro game be too much?

Because of the controversies in which Cam Newton was wrapped while in college, he was being watched particularly closely as a rookie. Following the NFL draft, many scouts and football analysts marveled over Newton's skillset. Others were sure he would fail, calling him immature, selfish, and entitled. Newton, it seemed, would not just need to prove his ability to play football. He needed to prove to all those who questioned his worth that he even belonged. ESPN polled fans the day after the NFL draft, asking, "Which of the first-round picks is a potential bust?" A whopping 77 percent of fans said "Cam Newton."

Some of the concerns were legitimate. Newton was known to have an imperfect throwing motion. And, because he was well

Opposite: Cam Newton entered his rookie season with many questioning if his collegiate success would translate to the NFL.

protected and played for such a strong team in college, he often did not have to make difficult passes. As his wide receivers were often wide open, no one was totally sure he could fit the ball into small, tight spaces in the defense, as is often necessary in the NFL. Next, Newton had so much success in college because of his ability to run with the football. This alone affected the way his opponents' defenses would play against him. One reporter asked: "Newton was amazing against college defenses, but professional opponents would prove more stout. What would Newton look like if he couldn't bully his way to touchdown after touchdown? If NFL defenses made him change his playing style, could he?" And last, while Newton has often said his journey to professional football has shaped his character, the journey itself had some questioning if Newton could be consistent. After all, he played only one full year of major college football (in the Football Bowl Series division). He sure had a successful year with Auburn, but could he replicate that success?

The answers came slowly. The NFL was encountering a **lockout** in the offseason, so preseason practices did not start until the end of July. By then, Newton had signed a $22 million contract. During the preseason practices, Newton was—like always, it seemed—competing for a starting job. He was up against Jimmy Clausen, who had graduated from the University of Notre Dame a year earlier, in 2010, and was drafted in the second round. Head coach Ron Rivera said that technically Clausen would start as the number one quarterback, but both would have a chance to prove themselves in a "fair competition." In the first few days, Newton received mixed reviews. He showed flashes of his potential, but rookie mistakes were sprinkled in. Still, coach Rivera told reporters he had one word to describe his early impression of Newton: "Wow."

Newton's coaches were interested to see how he would fare in a game situation. Before the NFL season begins, each team usually plays four preseason games intended to help them get tuned up against real competition before the games count in the standings. Newton's first NFL preseason game was against the New York Giants. He completed 8 of 19 passes for 134 yards and no touchdowns. His coaches thought he did well, but not great. The story was the same for the remainder of the preseason, throughout which his coaches wavered on who the starter would be.

Named the Starter

It wasn't until September 2, 2011 that Rivera made his choice: Newton would be the starter. However, his coaches would be watching him closely. The work wasn't over; it was just beginning. "We didn't draft Cam to be the savior," Rivera said. "We drafted him to help lead this football team."

Newton led. He made his NFL debut against the Arizona Cardinals on September 11, 2011, the ten-year anniversary of the 9/11 terrorist attacks. Coincidentally, the Cardinals' home field was the site of Newton's victory in the College Football National Championship game just nine months earlier. With all eyes on him, Newton dazzled. He did score one touchdown running, but mostly it was Newton's ability as a passer that was impressive. Newton completed twenty-four of thirty-seven pass attempts, resulting in a total of 422 yards and two touchdowns. Those 422 passing yards were the most *ever* for a quarterback in his first NFL game. A veteran wide receiver and teammate, Steve Smith, marveled over Newton's performance, saying: "He was everything everybody didn't expect him to be. He was on point, he made some great runs, he made some

Cam Newton quickly earned the respect of his Carolina Panther teammates as he took command of the huddle.

great reads, made some fantastic throws. He made some throws out there that honestly as a receiver it made it easy to catch them." One sports columnist wrote: "It wasn't a debut, but a revelation."

However, the Panthers lost, 28-21, and that's all that Newton seemed to be thinking about after the game. "The last time I lost a game was at Navarro Junior College [while playing for Blinn]," he told reporters. "What do you want me to say, 'It feels great?' It is not a comfortable feeling for me."

The second week of the NFL season would provide Newton with another opportunity to prove he—and his team—had what it takes to win. The Green Bay Packers, who were the defending Super Bowl champions, were next on the Panthers' schedule. Newton again threw for more than 400 yards, outdoing his debut with 432 total passing yards, a passing touchdown, and a rushing touchdown. But again, the Panthers lost by seven points. Newton's impatience with losing grew, as he said: "We've just got to get it right. We're going to get it right. But I'm not the person to just sit up here and say, 'Well, we have next time.' I'm not that type of person. I want it right now, and I want to get it right now."

Coach Ron Rivera continued to be impressed and surprised with his rookie quarterback's performance. "This is a rookie quarterback that's learning and growing and getting better each opportunity he gets," Rivera said. "When we go back and really get to watch the tape, we'll see he missed a read here, he missed a throw here, but for the most part, he handled himself with the type of poise and composure you would not expect. He puts a lot of pressure on himself to be great. Win or lose, it's always about what else he could have done to help the team. It's kind of that window-versus-mirror thing: In a win, he looks out and sees who else is doing a great job; when we lose, he looks in the mirror."

Strong Finish

The Panthers had their ups and downs the rest of the season, suffering several tough losses, but Newton was mostly flying high. He got his team soaring toward the end of the season, as he seemed to settle into his role even more. The Panthers won four of their last six games. His team had a final record of six wins and ten losses, but Newton almost singlehandedly was making the Panthers must-see TV week in and week out. Newton set a record for the most rushing touchdowns by a quarterback in a single season with fourteen, in addition to his twenty-one passing touchdowns. By the end of the season, he had become the first player in league history to throw for 4,000 yards and rush for 500. These feats led to Newton being honored as the NFL Offensive Rookie of the Year, as he received forty-seven of the fifty votes.

The only person less-than-impressed with Newton's performance? Newton himself. "I don't think anyone's expectations of me will ever be as high as mine," he said. "I'm not surprised by anything I do. The only time I'm surprised is when I don't play to my potential."

Over the next several years in the NFL, Newton's results steadily improved. While it took only a couple of weeks to convince the football-watching world of his abilities on the field, he still wanted to be winning a lot more often.

In 2012, the Panthers won one more game than in the previous season, finishing with a 7–9 record. Newton's numbers were slightly less electric, but those playing close attention saw his growth.

Newton was more efficient and dependable with the football, as he had fewer turnovers during his second NFL season. His team relied on him less to rush with the ball after signing a new running back in the offseason, so Newton—while still a threat to run the football—was able to focus more energy on developing as a passer.

The 2013 season would be special for Newton, as it ended with his first playoff appearance. The Panthers finished the regular season with a 12–4 record, winning the National Football Conference's South division and earning a trip to the postseason. Newton was named to the Pro Bowl, which is the all-star game for the NFL. As always, the individual **accolades** were less meaningful to Newton; the season ended in disappointment as the Panthers lost in the first round of the playoffs to the San Francisco 49ers. Newton lamented after the game about the difficulty of seeing the season come to a close. "It's hard as a person, it's hard as a man, it's hard as an individual, it's hard … when you put so much into it and you don't get the production that you want out of it," Newton said. "I had a coach tell me right after the game, 'It's a bad ending to a great season,' and he was right."

In the offseason, Newton underwent surgery to tighten his ankle ligaments, which had been bothering him since his time at Auburn. The recovery time was four months, which caused Newton to miss training camp and the first preseason game. He was with the team just a short while as he suffered hairline fractures to some ribs during the third preseason game. He would miss the season-opener, then return for an impressive season debut in the Panthers' home-opener in week two.

Over the next several games, he impressed analysts with his ability to get rid of the ball quickly when under pressure and balance

Cam Newton developed a stronger passing game in the pro ranks than many anticipated would be possible.

his running game with his passing game. Newton had four games with at least two hundred passing yards, eighty rushing yards, multiple touchdown passes and a rushing touchdown—the most in NFL history. For his performance against the New Orleans Saints on December 7, 2014, Newton was named the NFC Offensive Player of the Week. Then, two days later, he was in a car accident in which he fractured two vertebrae in his lower back. He missed only one game and was back in time to lead his team to a victory that would secure the division title and a trip to the playoffs for the second season in a row. Then the Panthers won their first playoff game in nine seasons, beating the Arizona Cardinals despite Newton having a subpar game. In the next round, the Seattle Seahawks' defense proved to be too much for Carolina. Newton and the Panthers lost, 31–17, and their season was over.

Great Investment

On June 2, 2015, Newton signed a five-year contract worth $103.8 million, assuring he would remain in Carolina. His team had been on the brink of making it big in the past two seasons, and the Panthers' ownership wanted him to stay. But the question remained: Would the investment pay off? In short, the answer was yes.

Newton's play during the 2015 season led reporters, analysts, and football fans across the country to wonder if his was the best season *ever* by an NFL quarterback. The team went 15–1 in the regular season. And Newton's numbers were astronomical. He finished the season with forty-five total touchdowns (thirty-five passing, ten rushing), which is the seventh highest total of all time. In just his fifth season, Newton tied former San Francisco quarterback Steve Young atop the NFL's all-time list with forty-three rushing touchdowns; it took Young fifteen years to accomplish the same feat.

Newton also proved how smart and effective he had gotten on the field. Of the players with whom Newton shared a spot on the top-ten list for most touchdowns in a season, he had the third-lowest turnover rate. One analyst said, "Newton doesn't get credit for his football IQ and his decision making, but the numbers show he has made great strides in both areas while not sacrificing his playmaking ability." And Newton made all this progress on a team that lacked stars other than him. Newton himself accounted for 76.2 percent of his team's total yards.

Despite his personal success, Newton was showing the viewing public what a leader he was. One reporter called him the best leader in the NFL. "He's doing it with a youthful approach, treating football like the game that it is," the reporter wrote. "And this, too, should not come as a surprise. Newton's one season at Auburn was magical, largely because of his leadership. His teammates bought-in, and it resulted in great success."

Another reporter said Newton found the perfect fit for his style: "People who argued Newton would bust because of his character and intelligence were catastrophically wrong. If anything, his charismatic personality has made him a more effective leader of a team that seems to accept and cherish his swag."

After a magical regular season, the Panthers navigated their way to the biggest football game of the year. In the Divisional Round of the playoffs they again met last year's playoff foe, the Seattle Seahawks. The Panthers had a 31–0 lead at halftime, but the

Seahawks scrapped back in the second half. Carolina held on to win 31–24. Newton introduced the idea of "Big Mo" and its role in playoff victories. "The playoffs bring out, more than any other time, the impact of 'Big Mo,'" Newton said. "Momentum. We can't wait for no one [sic] to make plays for us."

Up next would be the Arizona Cardinals. Newton led the offense to an NFC Championship game record forty-nine points. Among his highlights of the day was an eighty-six-yard touchdown pass. Newton finished the day with four touchdowns—two passing and two rushing. With the 49–15 win, the Panthers were headed to the franchise's second-ever appearance in a Super Bowl. After the win, Newton said, "We've been dreaming about this moment since day one. Yeah, we're going to the Super Bowl. We are not going just to take pictures. We are trying to finish this thing off."

Newton was focused on the field. But off the field, Newton's individual accomplishments were being recognized at the highest level. His mix of playmaking abilities and leadership led to him being voted the NFL's Most Valuable Player. Newton offered a video acceptance speech, as he was busy preparing for the Super Bowl. Newton said: "It means so much, but not just for myself. To be the first person in Panthers history to win it—that's what I'm most proud about. I've received a lot of awards, but to be able to get this organization here, I'm really proud. We didn't get in this position by happenstance. It took years of hard work and dedication, and now we are reaping the benefits."

Eye on the Ultimate Prize

Newton's family was at the ceremony to accept the award on his behalf. Cam's father, once the man at the center of so much

Quotes On Cam

"God's not making another Cam Newton for a long time. He broke the mold when He made him."

—NFL Hall of Fame wide receiver Cris Carter

"He's got a rocket of an arm, which he has learned to harness. He can do things in the run game that no other quarterback, perhaps in the history of the game, can do."

—NFL Hall of Fame General Manager Bill Polian

"When Cam steps into that locker room and that huddle, everybody's chest gets a little bit more puffed out. Everybody believes a little bit more that we can get something done. That's what the great ones have."

—Two-time NFL Most Valuable Player Kurt Warner

"What he's done in the short time being an NFL quarterback has been awesome. It's the best word I can think of. He's been a great passer, he's been a great runner, he's been a great leader. You don't go 17–1 as a starting quarterback without being awesome, and that's what he's been this year without a doubt."

—Two-time Super Bowl Champion quarterback Peyton Manning on Newton's 2015 season

"He always had a strong will to self-identify who he is and appreciate his person. He never cared whether people enjoyed or appreciated that or not. He was who he was. He is who he is. That always propelled him forward."

—Cecil Newton, Cam Newton's father

"I love the way he plays, the energy, the passion. It's contagious."

—NFL Hall of Fame coach Don Shula

A determined Denver Broncos defense rattled Cam Newton and the Carolina Panthers in the Super Bowl.

Cam Newton: Trying to Win Them All

controversy, offered his gratitude. "Cam took an unconventional journey to get here and we're just so proud of what has happened, my family and I," Cecil Newton said. "So many thanks go out to so many people, from Pop Warner to the Panthers. I don't have time to tell you all, 'thank you.' You know who you are. We know who you are."

The award was meaningful to Newton, but he had his eyes on one final prize, which so far he hadn't laid hands on: the Lombardi Trophy, which is awarded to the team that wins the Super Bowl.

The Super Bowl was set for Sunday, February 7, 2016, at Levi's Stadium in Santa Clara, California. The day will go down in infamy for the Carolina Panthers and Cam Newton, who could not overcome the Denver Broncos' suffocating defense. The Broncos were winning, 10–0, by the end of the first quarter and took a 13–7 edge into halftime. While the score never got out of hand, Carolina had such difficulty on offense that it seemed clear the Panthers would never bounce back. Newton got poor protection from his offensive line, as he was **sacked** six times. Newton also was responsible for three turnovers: one interception and two lost fumbles, one of which led to a Broncos touchdown. The final score was 24-10. Newton completed only eighteen of forty-one pass attempts for a total of 265 yards. He rushed six times for forty-five yards.

After the game, Newton had little interest in talking about the loss. He spoke with reporters for about five minutes and received much criticism for being so curt. He offered these words to conclude the season: "They just played better than us. I don't know what you want me to say. I'm sorry. They made more plays than us, and that's what it came down to. We had opportunities. It wasn't nothing [sic] special that they did. We dropped balls. We turned the ball over. We gave up sacks, threw errant passes. That's it. They scored more points than us."

Newton's storybook season had come to an end. While the final game didn't turn out as he wanted, nothing could take away from what he had done on the field all season, and throughout his entire NFL career.

Chapter 5

Giving Kids a Chance

Cam Newton's name will immediately bring to mind many football-related feats: Heisman Trophy winner, BCS National Champion, NFL MVP and, maybe one day, Super Bowl winner. But these honors aren't the only things that drive Newton in his daily work. Leaving his mark on the NFL is important to him, but so is leaving his mark on the world.

Newton hopes to be known as more than a football player. One of the major ways Newton has sought to have an impact is through his work with children. To be able to influence children on a regular basis, Newton created the Cam Newton Foundation, which according to its website is "committed to enhancing the lives of youth by addressing their educational, physical, and social needs." The overarching theme of the foundation is "Every 1 Matters" with a focus on areas of Every 1 Learns, Every 1 Plays, and Every 1 Gives.

One point of emphasis is to give disadvantaged children a chance to achieve their educational goals. Newton knows he was lucky to grow up in a household where education was emphasized—

Opposite: Cam Newton spends much of his free time helping many causes that improve the lives of children.

and he also knows not all children have the same luck. "When I was growing up, my parents really influenced me," Newton said. "But there are kids who don't have that type of influence. They need someone who can create avenues for their dreams—whether they want to be a football player, a doctor or a veterinarian." The foundation provides financial support and aid for motivated youth who may not have the resources to pursue their academic passions. Mentoring and tutoring programs are also available.

Focusing on play is important to Newton because he learned the values of teamwork, dedication, confidence, and physical fitness through his experiences on the football field. He wants all children to have access to this opportunity. With this in mind, Newton and his foundation are improving and revitalizing underserved communities by refurbishing neighborhood parks, fields, playgrounds, and community centers.

The focus on giving is inherent in everything Newton does. The foundation emphasizes volunteer work and the development of holiday outreach programs, so those in need can still have bright spirits even if they wouldn't otherwise have the resources.

Big Heart

Also, Newton loves a good surprise. In December 2015, a group of children were invited to a sporting goods store for what they thought was a holiday-season field trip. They knew they were being recognized for doing something important—improving their grades or their in-school behavior. What they didn't know was that quarterback Cam Newton would be there to celebrate with and encourage them. He watched as each of the children received $200 to spend on presents for themselves and their families. Gina Salvati, the vice president of advancement at Communities in Schools, had organized the event and was blown away by Newton's presence. "Cam has—and I don't know if the world knows this—a genuine heart for kids," Salvati said. "It's not just about the press or what he's supposed to do. It's about the way he wants to support kids and the way he wants them to be supported. Many of our kids really feel apart from the world; this is the way our kids can feel part of the world beyond their street."

Since 2013, Newton and his foundation have hosted "Cam's Thanksgiving Jam," which serves a traditional Thanksgiving meal to hundreds of underprivileged children. The events are not something Newton does for publicity—he truly enjoys them. In 2015, Newton hosted a "dab" contest, inviting children up on stage to perform his signature dance alongside him. In 2016, a DJ, face painting, and balloon artists were also part of the event. "To see the kids, to see the parents come out and to share a plate, share a moment, share a conversation with them, is always beneficial to both parties," Newton said. "Not only for them, but for me as well."

For Newton, it's not about hearing words of appreciation from those he spends time with. Oftentimes, he cherishes interactions with those who can't voice their gratitude. Before Christmas in 2015, Newton visited a school that works with children who are developmentally disabled, some of whom can't communicate verbally. Newton took the time to greet each child, taking pictures and selfies, hopefully reaching those who couldn't express their appreciation for his visit.

Lots of celebrities are looked at suspiciously for doing good deeds because people question their **motives**. Do they just want

One of Cam Newton's trademarks is giving a football to a child in the stands after his team scores a touchdown.

Cam Newton: Trying to Win Them All

Giving Kids a Chance

the good publicity? Are they showing support for others because cameras are on? Because Cam Newton is a celebrity, cameras are often on. However he performs good deeds all the time. In August of 2016, Newton was seen giving back—when he thought no one was watching. He and some teammates were leaving a restaurant when he came upon a homeless man with a sign that read "Please help. Hungry." Newton took a full meal and handed it to the man, clearly trying to be discreet. A woman named Candace Gregory happened to be going for a walk at the time and captured Newton's gesture with a photograph. "People talk about him dabbing and all the stuff that in my mind ultimately should be irrelevant, because that doesn't get to the heart of who he is," Candace said of Newton. "I once saw him give something to a disabled child at a practice and people were like, 'Oh, it's a photo opportunity.' But this was when nobody was looking. That's why we shared it, because character is what you do when nobody is looking."

While the Cam Newton Foundation is out in the public for all to see, even the foundation's director has been impressed with the role Newton takes in leading the organization toward its goal. For example, Newton has come up with ideas on how to raise funds for children in need. As Newton isn't much of a golfer, he decided to have a kickball tournament, which ultimately raised $300,000 for the foundation. Newton works hard to stay connected to his fans. The foundation's website has a section called "Ask Cam Anything," and each month he responds to questions about everything from his favorite food to his biggest pet peeve to if he enjoyed his offseason trip to Australia.

All In

Recently, Newton took on a new **venture**. In the fall of 2016, Newton debuted in a TV show on Nickelodeon called "All In With Cam Newton." The **premise** of the show is that Newton will help kids fulfill their dreams the same way people helped him reach his goals. Newton will surprise a child or two in each episode, ask them their goals and then pair them with a mentor who will help them work toward achieving that goal. The kids share aspirations ranging

In 2016, episodes of *All In With Cam* starting airing. Cam Newton spends time with children looking to achieve a goal.

from riding a BMX bike over ramps to making cakes or inventing apps. Jeff Sutphen, an actor/producer working on the show, has marveled over Newton's presence and demeanor in his work with children. "I just see how he's able to come in and relate to every kid," Sutphen said. "No matter what their area of expertise is, he's got something they can tie it back to and relate to his career and his upbringing and how he got to where he is. That's his big thing. He wants to say, 'Hey, I had help getting to where I am. I want to see if I can return that favor and help these kids get to where they want to be.'"

Newton reflected on superheroes and how they inspired him in the show's development. "When you look at comic books, and when you look at different superheroes, they all possess something different. Spider-Man wasn't like Superman. Superman wasn't like Wonder Woman. Wonder Woman wasn't like Aquaman. Aquaman wasn't like the Hulk. They all brought something different." Newton, in other words, doesn't want all kids to try to be just like him. He wants them to discover their own inner superhero.

Newton has since reflected on the experience of shooting the show—just after his Super Bowl loss, at that. He understands that his time as a star in the NFL will be limited to twenty years at a maximum. While he can build a second career on finding ways to give back through his foundation, and through other outlets, his presence *right now* means so much because of his star power. "Oftentimes it's healthy for people to try to get away, but while I'm relevant, I want to maximize my words to giving back," Newton said. "This felt like me giving back to the community, but it wasn't necessarily my community as it was giving back to the younger generation."

Cam Newton Scorecard

Career Highlights: Quarterbacked Auburn University's BCS National Champion team (2010); made three Pro Bowls (2011, 2013, 2015); led Panthers to NFL's best record of 15–1 (2015); led Panthers to NFC Championship and a berth in Super Bowl 50, where they were the runner-up (2015); set NFL rookie all-time record for passing and rushing yards (2011); set record for most rushing touchdowns (44) by a quarterback in NFL history (2016).

Firsts: First player in modern era to be awarded Heisman Trophy (2010), win BCS national championship (2010), and become the first overall pick in an NFL draft (2011); first quarterback to throw for 400 yards in his first NFL game; first NFL quarterback to throw for 4,000 yards in his rookie season; first NFL quarterback to throw for at least thirty touchdowns and rush for ten in the same season (2015).

Honors: NFL Most Valuable Player (2015); NFL All-Pro First Team (2015); NFL Rookie of the Year (2011); Heisman Trophy Winner (2010); Best NFL Player ESPY Award (2016); Bert Bell Award (2015); eight-time NFC Offensive Player of the Week; AP College Football Player of the Year (2010); Maxwell Award winner (2010), Walter Camp Award winner (2010), Davey O'Brien Award winner (2010), Manning Award winner (2010); consensus first-team All-American (2010).

Some of Newton's ambitions about "giving back" are grand. Others are small and spur-of-the-moment. Newton always has seemed to show respect and love for those who love the game like he does. In April 2016, he was driving in his car past the Community School of Davidson in North Carolina when he spotted a kid wearing his jersey. As a professional athlete, Newton sees people wearing his jersey all the time. However, this kid happened to be throwing a football. Newton wanted to join the game. After asking the teacher's permission, the star quarterback hopped over the fence and had a toss with some very lucky seventh-graders.

The theme to Newton's **philanthropic** activities is intentional. While Newton is known for his childlike nature at times, the fact is he loves children. For example, while at Blinn College, the then twenty-year-old Newton accompanied the son of his head coach, Brad Franchione, to kindergarten. "[Cam] was show-and-tell for my son's kindergarten class. He had the letter 'Q,' so he brought Cam, for quarterback," Franchione said. Also, since entering the NFL, Newton has become well known for distributing balls to children in the stands after he scores a touchdown.

Finding Balance in Life

Recently, Newton became focused on one child in particular: his own. In December 2015, Newton's girlfriend, Kia Proctor, gave birth to a boy whom they named Chosen Sebastian Newton. Newton's love for his son is obvious. He also shows his sense of humor when discussing parenting and how quickly his little boy is growing. "He does have scholarship offers," Newton told ESPN, with a smile. "Now, I [don't] mean to be rude or ask anybody who has any daughters, but he's trying to sign some type of agreement right now for first dibs on prom invite, so he's a busy guy. Man, it's crazy. I was thinking about taking little Chosen to the DMV about getting his license. It's about that time. He texted me yesterday and said he wanted to work out … two-a-days and stuff like that. I have my hands full."

Newton also reflected on ways in which having a son has changed him. At one time, he wanted to live a happy life with everything he needed, of course. But his ambition and drive have grown. The goal "was always to live comfortably and do the things that you want to do with whoever you want to do it with," he said. "Now it's like, you have a seed on this earth that you see all your similarities in, from the nose, the ears, the face, the smile. You know, the body composition, and everything just makes you feel obligated to make his life as easy as possible." Having a son has also helped him ignore his critics. He told one reporter that others can say what they want about him, but as long as his son isn't the one offering the criticism, it won't hurt so much. "That's what the birth of my son does. Like, what do I gain? Now I have purpose in this world. Whether a mean tweet, a mean [person] saying, 'Hey, you're supposed to do it like this'—if my son ain't [sic] saying it, then it don't [sic] matter to me."

Newton has sometimes been criticized for the passion he displays while playing, but to others he is a reminder that we should all care about doing our best and trying to see results. One sportswriter wrote that Cam's passion for the game should seem familiar to everyone watching because "Cam is simply a football fan playing football." The writer continues: "Cam is emotional. What you call showboating, Cam calls celebrating. What you call sulking, Cam calls reacting. What you call cocky, Cam calls confidence. Cam is naturally emotional, and he has no interest in hiding his emotion. You scream at your team, tear off your jersey, and threaten a kicker over a missed field goal. Cam dabs when he scores touchdowns, collapses on the sideline when his team loses, and is unable to put on a happy face immediately after a devastating loss. He has highs and lows, just like you. And like all fanatics, his highs are the highest and his lows are the lowest." Newton expects greatness of himself and his team because he knows that fans expect that of him.

Newton seems to accept that his passion for winning—and disdain for losing—will be part of his legacy. These qualities are built into the very fabric of who he is. And losing the Super Bowl? He still carries that heart-wrenching defeat with him. "The optimism of football brings people together closer than any other sport," he said. "It's all about winning. … I just hate that we didn't win."

It is clear that Newton loves to win and loves his work with children, but that doesn't mean he has shied away from more serious topics as he builds his legacy. Newton also has hypothesized that his actions are questioned by some for a much deeper reason: his race. "I'm an African American quarterback that scares people because they haven't seen nothing [sic] that they can compare me to," Newton said. "I don't think people have seen what I am or what I'm trying to do." One sportswriter who covers the Panthers, Jonathan Jones, wrote that Newton's behavior may be misunderstood because non-black viewers misunderstand him and his culture. "Newton is a young, successful, black man celebrating through culturally relevant means," Jones wrote. Meanwhile, Ozzie Newsome, a Hall of Fame tight end who is also black, reflected on the relevance of having black star quarterbacks today. "I was a pretty good quarterback growing up, but when it came to organized football, I knew I should become

Cam Newton balances his professional life with his family. He and girlfriend Kia Proctor welcomed a son, Chosen Sebastian Newton, in December 2015.

a wide receiver because from everything that I was reading, all the blacks were getting their positions changed," Newsome said. "Now you've got some heroes that you can look at; there is someone you can **emulate** who is black."

In the Minority

Newton remains among the minority of quarterbacks who are African American; there were only five black starting quarterbacks as of the beginning of the 2016 NFL season. However, in a *GQ* article about him, Newton said the venom toward him wasn't about race, "We're beyond that. As a nation." He has somewhat backtracked, or clarified, what he meant and has since used his public platform to share his thoughts on the racial inequalities still present in the United States.

He has not, however, used his status in the same way other African American athletes have. For example, former San Francisco 49ers quarterback Colin Kaepernick has refused to stand during the national anthem at sporting events, as a sign of frustration about the treatment of minorities in the United States. "I am not going to stand up to show pride in a flag for a country that oppresses black people and people of color," Kaepernick said.

Newton voiced support for Kaepernick for making the stand the way he has. However, Newton offered a different perspective in an Instagram post that said: "The real problem is and will always be the people, and how we treat one another. ... I'm an African American that's black and proud to the day I die, and I try to make an impact in my community as much as I can. How are you making a difference? But it all goes for nothing if we all don't police ourselves and love one another no matter what the race is. We all have to do better and be held accountable for our actions (police included). ... I'm not here to talk about race, I'm here to talk about what's right. And we all have to do what's right no matter the race, age, or gender."

In his role as the face of an NFL franchise, Newton carries many responsibilities. The first, most obvious task to which he has dedicated himself is that of winning. He commits himself to improving, leading, and helping those around him perform at their best. But as a public figure, Newton has shown that he understands there is more for him to accomplish off the football field, too. For better or worse, many children look up to superstar athletes, and Newton seems to appreciate that his job is to act like someone who children should want to emulate. He is generous with his money and his time, seeking to better the lives of those around him, particularly children.

If Newton were to retire tomorrow, he already would be considered to have had an electric and successful career. He has come back from controversy at the college level to win a Heisman Trophy and a national championship. He was chosen No. 1 in the NFL draft by the Carolina Panthers and quickly proved that those who doubted that he would succeed were wrong, as he was named NFL Offensive Rookie of the Year. He led his team to the peak of the professional game, when the Carolina Panthers went to the Super Bowl in his fifth season at the helm. And he continues working every day to bring them back—so he can win this time.

Timeline

May 11, 1989 Cameron Jerrell Newton is born in College Park, Georgia.

1996 Cam Newton plays football for the first time.

Fall 2003 Newton makes Westlake High School debut as a freshman after first- and second-string quarterbacks are injured, and he fumbles near the goal line in loss to Mays.

Fall 2005 Newton becomes a star during his junior season at Westlake High School.

September 8, 2006 Newton commits to the University of Florida.

November 21, 2008 Newton is arrested for allegedly stealing another student's laptop; he is suspended from the Florida football team.

January 5, 2009 Newton announces he is transferring to Blinn College in Brenham, Texas.

December 6, 2009 Newton leads Blinn to the NJCAA National Championship with a 31–26 victory over Fort Scott (Kansas).

December 31, 2009 Newton announces he will transfer to Auburn University.

December 13, 2010 Newton awarded the Heisman Trophy.

January 10, 2011 Newton and the Auburn Tigers win the BCS national championship by beating Oregon in the title game.

January 13, 2011 Cam Newton declares for the NFL draft, ending his playing career at Auburn.

April 28, 2011 Newton is chosen with the No. 1 pick of the NFL draft by the Carolina Panthers

September 11, 2011 Newton becomes the first rookie quarterback to throw for 400 yards in a season-opener.

February 4, 2012 Newton honored as NFL Offensive Rookie of the Year.

December 22, 2013 Newton and the Panthers clinch a playoff berth with a victory over the New Orleans Saints. It is the first playoff berth in Newton's NFL career.

January 3, 2015 Newton wins his first playoff game as the Panthers defeat the Arizona Cardinals, 27–16.

December 24, 2015 Newton becomes a father as girlfriend Kia Proctor gives birth to their son Chosen.

February 6, 2016 Newton is named NFL Most Valuable Player.

February 7, 2016 Newton and the Panthers lose in Super Bowl L to the Denver Broncos, 24–10.

Glossary

accolades Awards or honors given to acknowledge achievement.

alumni Graduates or former students of a school, college, or university.

amateurism The practice of a person who engages in a sport and has not gained any financial benefit above his or her actual and necessary expenses. This includes scholarship athletes.

center An offensive lineman who positions himself in the middle of the line and puts the ball into play by snapping the ball to the quarterback.

collegiate Of or relating to a college or its students.

divisiveness A tendency to causing strong disagreement, discord, or hostility among people or groups.

dual-threat A description of a quarterback who possesses the skills to both run and pass effectively.

eligibility Having the right to play a sport or to stay in school by satisfying certain conditions.

emulate To try to equal or surpass, usually by imitation.

first down Maintaining possession of the football for another set of a maximum four downs or plays either by gaining 10 yards (9.1 m) in the previous set of downs or by penalty on the defense.

five-star prospect A high school athlete receiving the maximum grade by scouts, coaches, or analysts.

intangibles Qualities or attributes that can't be touched or objectively measured, such as will or inner drive.

linebacker A defensive player who lines up behind players on the line of scrimmage but in front of the defensive secondary.

lockout The temporary closing of a business because of a disagreement between the employer and the employees over working conditions.

motive Something that causes a person to act in a certain way.

nominees Persons named as candidates for consideration for a position or an award.

offensive coordinator The person who designs and manages a football team's entire offense, both running and passing.

philanthropic Showing concern for human welfare and advancement and supporting those things with financial resources.

preeminent Superior to all others in a field or profession; distinguished.

premise The statement from which a conclusion is to be drawn.

reinstated Restored to a position or condition, or put back in force such as a law.

rookie An athlete playing his or her first season, usually in a professional sport.

sack To tackle the quarterback behind the line of scrimmage before the quarterback can pass the ball.

scrutiny A critical examination or investigation of a person or an organization.

tutelage The guidance, instruction, or protection of a person.

venture An undertaking that may have an uncertain outcome.

versatility Having the ability to adapt to or perform many different functions.

Further Information

Books

Blattenberger, Phil, and Brad Mills. *Fifteen and 1: An Unofficial and Unfiltered History of Professional Football in Carolina*. Charlotte, NC: Madison Press, 2016.

Charlotte Observer. *Super Cam: Cam Newton's Rise to Panthers Greatness*. Chicago: Triumph Books, 2016.

Heisman, John M., and Mark Schlabach. *Heisman: The Man Behind the Trophy*. Brentwood, TN: Howard Books, 2012.

Websites

Auburn's Cam Newton Timeline

http://www.al.com/sports/index.ssf/2010/12/auburns_cam_newton_timeline_fr.html
Follow the events surrounding Cam Newton's recruitment and arrival at Auburn University.

The Cam Chronicles

http://www.espn.com/espn/eticket/story?page=camnewton&num=1
Five writers for ESPN contribute to the story of Cam Newton from high school into the future.

Official Cam Newton Website

https://www.cam1newton.com
This site provides information on Cam Newton the football player and the foundation he started to help children.

Pro Football Reference

Cam Newton

http://www.pro-football-reference.com/players/N/NewtCa00.htm

This excellent source for statistics gives you Cam Newton by the numbers.

Videos

Cam Newton Dab Highlights

https://www.youtube.com/watch?v=wynkJV802MU
View this collection of Cam Newton big-play celebrations, including his dab.

Cam Newton Highlights MVP

https://www.youtube.com/watch?v=cAN0ZZnMLe8
Watch Carolina Panthers quarterback Cam Newton make play after play during his 2015 NFL MVP season.

Cam Newton—2010-11 Highlights

https://www.youtube.com/watch?v=p2vbPJJL5Pg
Watch the highlights from Cam Newton's championship season at Auburn University.

Cam Newton Wins the 2010 Heisman

https://www.youtube.com/watch?v=HLhr4b2HzHc
This video shows the 2010 Heisman Trophy presentation.

Bibliography

Books

Charlotte Observer. *Super Cam: Cam Newton's Rise to Panthers Greatness.* Chicago, IL: Triumph Books, 2016.

Coach Jeff. *Cam Newton Quiz Book.* Amazon Digital Services LLC, 2014.

Fishman, Jon M. *Cam Newton.* Minneapolis: Lerner Publications, 2016.

Holmes, Parker. *Football's Rising Stars: Cam Newton.* New York, NY: PowerKids Press, 2012.

Johnson, Joe. *Cam Newton: The NFL Star's Life and Career.* Amazon Digital Services LLC, 2013.

Online Articles

Associated Press. "Auburn releases Cam Newton docs." ESPN.com. November 5, 2011. http://www.espn.com/college-football/ story/_/id/7190987/auburn-tigers-records-reveal-details-cam-newton-scandal

————— "Florida's Newton faces felony counts after fellow student's laptop stolen." ESPN.com. November 21, 2008. http://www. espn.com/college-football/news/story?id=3718266

Baron, Zach. "Cam Newton on Those Versace Pants, Race in America, and Whether He Would Let His Kid Play Football." *GQ.* August 15, 2016. http://www.gq.com/story/cam-newton-versace-pants-race-and-football

Barrows, Frank. "Barrows on Sports: The Making of Cam Newton." *Charlotte Magazine*. August 23, 2012. http://www. charlottemagazine.com/Charlotte-Magazine/September-2012/ Barrows-on-Sports-The-Making-of-Cam-Newton/index. php?cparticle=2&siarticle=1#artanc

Baskin, Ben. "An oral history of the star-studded 2011 NFL draft, five years later." *Sports Illustrated*. April 26, 2016. http://www. si.com/nfl/2016/04/26/2011-nfl-draft-oral-history-cam-newton-von-miller

Cameron, Ryan. "Cam Newton's High School Coach Talks About The Early Years Of The Super Bowl Quarterback." V103 CBS Local. February 3, 2016. http://v103.cbslocal. com/2016/02/03/cam-newtons-former-hs-coach-dallas-allen-talks-about-cams-growth-into-a-man

Duart, Joseph. "Newton Found Refuge at Blinn Before Heading to Auburn." *Houston Chronicle*. November 15, 2010. http://www. chron.com/sports/college/article/Newton-found-refuge-at-Blinn-before-heading-to-1703666.php

ESPN Staff. "The Cam Chronicles." ESPN.com. Accessed November 15, 2016. http://www.espn.com/espn/eticket/ story?page=camnewton

Fowler, Jeremy. "Cam Newton left Florida Gators wondering what could have been." ESPN.com. September 17, 2015. http://www. espn.com/college-football/story/_/id/13657212/cam-newton-left-florida-gators-teammates-wondering-lost-potential

Goldberg, Charles. "Auburn's Cam Newton timeline: From recruitment to NCAA ruling." Alabama Media Group. December 1, 2010. http://www.al.com/sports/index.ssf/2010/12/ auburns_cam_newton_timeline_fr.html

Klein, Gary. "Auburn defeats Oregon, 22-19, to win BCS national championship game." *Los Angeles Times*. January 10, 2011. http://articles.latimes.com/2011/jan/10/sports/la-sp-bcs-championship-live11

Nusbaum, Eric. "The House that Built Cam." Vice Sports. February 5, 2016. https://sports.vice.com/en_us/article/the-house-that-built-cam

Sampson, Kirk. "Cam Newton: 2010 Heisman Trophy Winner." AuburnTigers.com. April 13, 2012. http://www.auburntigers.com/sports/m-footbl/spec-rel/041312aal.html

Schlabach, Mark. "Cam Newton puts stamp on title game." ESPN.com. December 4, 2010. http://www.espn.com/college-football/columns/story?id=5885469&columnist=schlabach_mark

Sherman, Rodger. "Let's remember all the people who said Cam Newton was too stupid and dishonest to succeed in the NFL." SB Nation. February 6, 2016. http://www.sbnation.com/2016/2/6/10883780/lets-remember-all-the-people-who-said-cam-newton-was-too-stupid-and

Thamel, Pete. "Heisman Front-Runner is Focus of Investigation." *New York Times*. November 4, 2010. http://www.nytimes.com/2010/11/05/sports/ncaafootball/05auburn.html

Index

About the Author

Jackie F. Stanmyre is a social worker and writer. She won awards as a newspaper reporter at the *Star-Ledger* of Newark, New Jersey before beginning a new career in mental health and addictions treatment. As an author for Cavendish Square Publishing, she has written for the Dangerous Drugs, Game-Changing Athletes, It's My State! and Primary Sources of the Abolitionist Movement series. Jackie lives in New Jersey with her husband and son.